How to Deal with Negative People

Protect Your Boundaries, Build Confidence, And Gain Respect

By

Bob Scott

Copyright © Bob Scott – All rights reserved.

No part of this publication shall be reproduced, duplicated or transmitted in any way or by any means, digital or otherwise, including photocopying, scanning, uploading, recording and translating or by any information storage or retrieval system, without the written consent of the author.

Table of Contents

INTRODUCTION 7
HOW TO RECOGNIZE NEGATIVE PEOPLE 9
CONTROLLING YOUR EMOTIONS 17
CONTROLLING YOUR ANGER 20
HOW TO EXPRESS ANGER 23
THINGS TO AVOID WHEN EXPRESSING ANGER 25
DEALING WITH NEGATIVE PEOPLE 27
HOW TO HANDLE CHALLENGE ELEGANTLY 35
HOW TO PROTECT YOUR BOUNDARIES 41
IMPROVE YOUR SELF-ESTEEM 49
HOW TO EARN RESPECT 58
CONCLUSION 63

Positive thoughts bring about positive response even to unpleasant actions. When you exhibit a strong positivity, you overpower the potential of any negative action around you.

Most of us don't experience the pleasure of solving problems because we are busy running away from them.

Surround yourself with people with whom you find relevance. They have to be interested in your progress and be fascinated by your charm.

INTRODUCTION

Negative people take pleasure in bringing your spirit down. They might pose as friends, but deep inside they are selfish, self-centered and angry with themselves. They don't want to see you enjoy things, of course, because they can't enjoy it. They aim to project their sadness to other people, and when you have a good heart, you are the most vulnerable target.

You will meet negative people in all areas of life. Starting from relationships, family, or even the workplace, you will always meet someone with a less-than-positive personality traits. But you don't have to be stressed about them anymore. You can still be compassionate and energetic and subtly deal with negative people.

A negative person is also emotionally unstable and pessimistic. In some cases, they feel like they are doing the right thing, not knowing that their life is all about complaining about things happening around them. They blame people or situations for their mistakes. They never admit their weaknesses. Even when they do, they tend to be pessimistic about the idea for change or improvement.

If you are close to this person, your mood is always affected, and you will end up emotionally drained. It is hard to find motivation when someone is constantly complaining about work and how life is unfair. You've been running, avoiding and hiding for a while. But its time to face the problem and tackle it with full efficiency. The strategies explored in this book will help you in dealing with negative people, achieving emotional stability, and thriving socially like you own your space. After following the strategies, you will be unaffected by people's negativities. And you won't have to run or hide from them anymore. Negative people will be less engrossed to you, and you will finally gain your social freedom to explore all your potentials.

HOW TO RECOGNIZE NEGATIVE PEOPLE

Negative and fake people tend to have similar characteristics. Here are some of the social traits common among toxic and negative people.

Exclusion

They exclude you from their schedules without reason. This occurs when you are friends or in a relationship with that person. They exclude you especially when they have to meet or do some things with other friends.

They disappear when you need them the most

They are your friends when you have everything in abundance, joy, money, health, etc. but they bail out at the time they know you will need them. The positive friends, the real ones stay with you in your ups and downs. They get affected by your misery, and they show real concern.

They gossip about the other friend

They gossip about the other person. Even though they treat him as a friend in his presence, they trash him in his absence. If they gossip about the other friend or talk badly about them, imagine what they would say about you with other people. This kind of people lack loyalty, and they can't be genuine with you if they are not genuine with the so-called friend.

Get you in trouble

They always have a reason to do something illegal or not totally humane. They influence you to do things you wouldn't normally do because your parents raised you well. Even if you are at the brink of making bad decisions, they don't make an effort to stop you. They don't offer emotional support when you need one but may suggest a deadly action that you might end up regretting afterwards.

They share your secrets

They use friendly blackmail to get things from you. Sometimes if you refuse to cave in, they playfully tell people your secrets.

They expose your secrets and still manage to make their actions look cool and unoffensive. A true friend will not tell others your secret, and wouldn't want you to suffer the emotional trauma of being blackmailed by another person, talk more of themselves.

They are unreliable

They don't take that action a friend should take at necessary times. They change easily, and you cannot rely on them in times of emergencies. You do the work of the friendship, and they remain on the receiving side. You know it within your mind that you cannot rely on this person, yet you are still friends.

Friendship with conditions

Your friendship is seasonal and has to come with conditions. You have a relationship with this person, but you get treated with compassion only when they are in a good mood, or when you have done something extraordinarily impressive. Your actions have to earn their compassion and sympathy, even empathy.

Certainly, a backbiter

You've heard so many times about the bad things they've been saying about you, and they keep denying. There is no mutual respect, even when you try as much as possible to create one. They don't seem to care much about the essence of details and being positive about someone even when they are not around.

They are full of drama

They have drama, and always want to include you in their dramas. They are negative about a lot of things, and they complain about things that are irrelevant to the cause of their pains. They create a scene and make your life miserable just because they are having a rough day. They shout and throw things because they think their feelings matter the most, more than anything else.

They don't celebrate with you

They don't congratulate you when good things happen to you. They are negatively competitive. They envy you but silently. In this case, the person doesn't have to be less achieving than you are to be envious. They can be very successful and still envy your lesser success. They tend to care less about your happiness, and even feel left out when you are happier than them.

Too competitive

These people are aggressively competitive. Competition is a normal way of life once a while, but being competitive about everything, to the extent of making the other person look bad because you want to look better, is a whole new level of social toxicity. The manipulations are of toxic forms. Overall, the relationship or friendship is never healthy, and you should deal with the negativity or find a way to get away from the person.

Spending time with them feels horrible

You feel like you have wasted time whenever you spend some minutes with them. There is a negative feeling that follows you whenever you interact with this person. Sometimes your emotions respond to things faster than your thinking. Your conscious mind may not figure out the problem, but your emotions are affected because there is definitely a problem.

A friendship or relationship should be fulfilling. You should want to meet that person, and even miss them immediately you are apart. If you are not getting any benefit, then you don't have a healthy relationship with this person.

They make fun of you in front of others

They call you names or despise you around other people. They don't regard you as an equal, or someone who is important. They throw you under the bus in awkward or challenging situations. They use sarcasm to hurt your feelings to satisfy their need to look cool.

This negative behavior comes from a negative angle or thinking pattern. They don't feel good about themselves, so they try as much as possible to project the negative feelings to someone else, and you tend to be the perfect target.

They don't listen

Your conversation is all about listening to them talking about themselves, career, business, or their neighbor. They barely listen to you or give attention to what is happening in your life.

They are practically self-centered and narcissistic, even though they like to put their nose in another person's business. You are the only one with good listening skill, and they just keep talking and leave when they are tired.

They only get in touch when they need something

You are irrelevant to them when their life is going well, but they come to you as soon as things go south. They might not even pick or return your calls, but they expect you to take immediate action to take care of them when they are in need.

Constant blamers

They blame other people for their mistakes. When you confront them about a wrongdoing, they blame you for putting them in the position to do such act. They do not accept fault, and they thrive well in arguments. They can argue all day about an irrelevant topic just to prove they are right.

They are good at sabotaging things

They obstruct a good conversation for something silly just to get the attention to themselves. They hate serenity, often professionally unstable. They undermine the importance of agreements, deadlines, official activities, projects, office tasks, etc. The resent over the pettiest and silly things.

Apparently, some of the things mentioned above might be a part of behavior that construes a lack of social skill. But you have to be careful, not to confuse arrogance with ignorance. If you are an adult who learned a decent moral skill and you can realize when things are not normal, the other person supposed to know the same thing. So, you are not responsible for feeling sorry for them. Cut this person off, and if you have to relate or work with them to achieve your purpose, use the strategies exposed in this book to deal with negative people.

CONTROLLING YOUR EMOTIONS

You cannot control anger if you can't control your emotions. Here are some tricks to control your emotions in overwhelming situations.

Gratefulness

Being grateful means focusing on the right things that are happening to you instead of the wrong ones. It also entails being positive about the less flattering sides of your life and the people around you. A grateful person remembers all the great things happening and does not complain much about the negative things. There is a peace of mind that is deep, unaltered by the behaviors or actions of people around him.

Laugh more

Laughing is the greatest medicine for humankind. Laughter regulates the stress response of the body. Exposing yourself to laugh creates a healthy emotional state. You will begin to have a healthy perspective about people, your life, and how to deal with problems that have to do with your social life. To laugh more, surround yourself with people who find it easier to laugh, and to enjoy life in all its glory. Surround yourself with positive minded people; those that will not bring trouble, only joy, and the reason to keep on smiling. Let go of those that tend to criticize your happiness. If they don't want you to be happy, they certainly don't deserve you.

Relax more

Practice various relaxation techniques to relieve physical and emotional stress. Do not allow yourself to stay in the work atmosphere for too long. Take time off people and work to enjoy some silence alone. Get away from the chaotic world, and focus on yourself through creative visualization or mindfulness meditation. There are different forms of relaxation according to your need. Some read books to relax, while others watch positive motivational movies. Others use yoga and other physical activities, sex, swim, etc.

Think of things that will relax your mind, and head for it.

CONTROLLING YOUR ANGER

Negative people can make you angry, and out of control sometimes. The best thing you can do is stay above them. Responding puts you in the same position with a toxic person. So, these are some tricks to deal with anger.

Talk about your feelings

The deadliest outrage is the one that is kept bottled up for a very long time. If you are not okay with how things are going, talk to someone you trust and express your feelings. You cannot deal with emotional dissatisfaction by repressing your feelings. Talk to a loved one, someone you know closely. The aim is not to look for a solution but to relieve the feeling by just talking about it. Knowing that someone listens and understands what we are going through solves 50 percent of the problem.

Stop the accusation

People are faulty, but naturally, no one will just accept the fall. If you are upset, keep calm and stay quiet for a minute or two. Never use the phrase "you make me upset." Do not blame others for your feelings. Do not accuse someone of making you feel bad about something. Do not allow them to think that they have power over your feelings. Express your feelings accordingly without making the next person feel like they have full responsibility for it.

Exercise

Sometimes working out helps you relieve anger. The aim is to channel the anger emotion into a healthy activity. Working out does not always mean going to the gym. You can always go for a walk, or take a jog around the block. Exercises help the brain and the body to relax, through the natural relieve of stress and anger emotions.

Stay still

Slowing down is very important especially when you realize your anger formed as a result of long-term mental or physical stress. Sometimes it is good to skip the email or the entire task to recalculate everything. You are not required to take any particular action when you read an upsetting message. Take a break from the computer for 20 to 30 minutes, and you will come back less angry and in control of the situation. You might choose not to respond at all, or respond in a more civilized manner, therefore making your business a success.

HOW TO EXPRESS ANGER

Here are some healthy ways to express anger:

Timeliness

As much as we are advised against expressing anger too early, we are also advised against expressing it too late or not expressing it at all. Your emotional state is one of the important variables that create your personality. The last thing you want to do is to allow a bottled-up feeling to ruin your endeavor. Anytime you feel like something is not going right in your relationship, look for the closest perfect time and express it. You don't have to use the angry tone while expressing your feelings, so you may not rush it. On the other hand, do not wait too long that your point or the feelings itself will seem irrelevant to the circumstance.

Go direct to the point

Do not cycle your point by bringing irrelevant details. Go direct to the point, and focus on the single thing that made you angry. The aim is to hit the nail right on the head. Doing otherwise will leave you frustrated and unsatisfied with the conversation. Your emotional turmoil will not improve until you can express your feelings. As much as you are talking to the person who makes you angry, focus on expressing your feelings and skip all other details.

Stay honest

Be honest about the details and about how you feel. You don't have to lie just to get sympathy. Instead of getting sympathy, you might end up looking vulnerable and weak. When you are hurting, let the person know you are hurting. If you cannot talk at the moment, you can simply walk away and talk only when you feel confident to do so. You cannot pretend to be angrier than you are, or less angry than you are. Let nature takes place for the effective expression of the anger emotion.

THINGS TO AVOID WHEN EXPRESSING ANGER

Long-term anger

Keeping your anger alive will only affect you, not the other person. Just as you can't laugh at the same joke all day, you can't be angry at the same thing all day. At some point, it is healthier to let go, than to keep on going on and on about how angry you are, and how the other person is negative and toxic. Give yourself a break by finding better ways to express your feelings. Being angry all the time will make you the negative person, not the other person. Choose peace. Make yourself happy by going to an environment that will not remind you of the negative deed.

Don't be too fast

If both of you are angry, expressing your anger will only lead to an argument. Even if you have to keep quiet and allow them to talk, you have to wait for better timing for correct expression. Do not argue with someone in a crowd, especially when you have to shout to be heard. Do not respond or impulsively run through the anger lane just because you are not comfortable. Master the art of timing, and you will never have to worry about the outcome of people's behavior toward you.

Don't be passive aggressive

Being passive aggressive may send the wrong signal as of the reason for your actions. Also, it makes the anger linger, which is a very unhealthy way to handle emotional situations. Avoid things like pouting, moodiness, grumpiness, backbiting, negative comments, silent treatment, etc., when you are angry with someone. Agree to talk to them, or even if they don't request, confront them about your feelings. This will help you get over the feeling, and you can concentrate on your life without hurting yourself or someone else.

DEALING WITH NEGATIVE PEOPLE

Work on your relationship

Realize that negative people are going to be negative, no matter the effort you put into creating a positive environment for them. Learn to let go when it is necessary. If they can't stop talking about the horrible things that happened to them, or the things they imagine could happen to them, take off. Simply, find a place where you will stay less in touch with this person for a while. You don't have to be with them all the time. Give yourself a break to be able to come back strong to put up with their negative ideas, perspectives, and approaches. Don't allow yourself to suffocate for too long around these people.

Do not react, act

Be a leader. Leadership does not react to circumstances. Leaders lead by action, not reaction. Do not respond to a negative person's depressed or angry dispositions.

The best thing you can do is to stay unaffected by the negative feelings and thoughts that are shared around by this person.

Act upon creating a positive perspective, circumstance, and even feelings, to replace the negative ones. Use simple rewards and compliments when they do something great. Appreciate them when they make a small effort to stay positive or achieve something they really want.

Sometimes people are negative because they think less of themselves, or they want to create a front for boldness when they are afraid deep inside. Whichever may be the case, always remain positive about them when they decide to do something positive and relevant. Do not react to their negativities., have a planned move, and follow the plan no matter what happens, what they say or do.

Let personal be personal

A person who is labeled as negative does not have to be wrong all the time. There are times they will tell you something harshly and using vulgar words. You shouldn't just brush off the comments and opinions. Learn to pick up the details. If they touched something sensitive about you, look into it, and try to improve if necessary.

We are not perfect, and sometimes people react according to our actions. It might be right for you, but once it irritates the other, there will never be a balance. Try and be the understanding one.

Appreciate them for pointing out the mistake, and assure them that you will take all necessary actions and that you are expecting them to take a particular step in similar situations. Two people taking a step for change and self-improvement is more promising than one.

Work with numbers

An apple doesn't fall far from the tree. A vine tree cannot sprout apple fruit. When a negative person is making life miserable for you and others, just be assured that they have a worse life. Be assured that you are doing better than him.

People tend to be totally negative because they can't think of or cultivate anything positive. You should be sorry for them, instead of blaming or fighting them. Actually, you should be motivated to help them. Start by making positive comments about them, using simple compliments. You don't necessarily have to support them, just don't allow yourself to be carried away by their negative behaviors.

Weigh the benefit

If you have to relate or work with a negative person, what do you get out of it?

The aim here is to look for a reason to stick around. If there is no reason, then you don't have to stick around anymore. Negative behavior can be a source of mental and physical stress. If the person is not making you money, creating a sort of comfort or family, you have to be honest with yourself and let go.

Write down the benefits of doing things with this person, and you will build the courage to manage and cope with their behaviors. Also, you will be able to act accordingly, and with grace, gain control of yourself and the things that concern you.

Control your empathy

People with strong emotions tend to attract negative people easily. A negative person loves to be around people who respond to them emotionally. They want to know that they affect people. So, if you are easily offended, outraged or compassionate towards people, a negative person will locate you easily and will stick around for a long period.

Learn to control your response towards a negative behavior. Control your reaction and physical response to the situation. Either change the subject or walk away. If they want you to be compassionate, give them a single response and leave.

Don't fix them, help them

Bear in mind that you cannot change people, no matter how hard you try. Do not go through the stress of trying to fix them. Be of help as much as you can for the moment, and let go.

Whenever a negative person starts talking about the things that are not right, and how the world is cruel, distract them with a positive topic about them, like their birthdays, families, work, or hobbies.

Make boundaries known

No matter how much you love that person, you must be clear about your boundaries. They must understand the meaning of your personal space and how they must not violate it. If you want to have control of your feelings, you have to learn to achieve control over your personal space.

Control starts from the space around you. Once the territory is under your control, you don't have to spend so much energy trying to deal with negative influences. The best you can do is to increase positivity, act according to your feelings, and try as much as possible to protect yourself and your feelings from negative people. You don't have to talk to them unless necessary.

Don't get entangled in the mess

You can ask them questions or take some steps to help their situation. But never get entangled in their mess. Knowing about the problem is important if you want to have a clear insight on how to solve them, but don't allow emotions to get in the way of your judgment.

Being entangled in the mess, you might find yourself skipping everything that matters to you, just to take care of the negative person. If they made the wrong choices, it is only fair if they face the consequences alone. It is very important to realize that consequences come as a result of bad actions. Your job is to allow an incentive for change to occur, without disrupting the natural moral flow.

Do not judge

Do not label someone so quickly; you might lose your real sense of empathy. Sometimes people don't turn out to be what we thought.

If you label a person as negative and toxic, they turn out to be the same thing even just to us. Some people may find them pleasant and okay to be with, but you may not.

No matter what you have been told about someone, do not assume they are completely bad. Make a personal assessment from the details you will obtain when you meet them. If they are tense, you are free to ask questions. With good understanding, you will realize that this person is not as bad as everyone label them to be.

Positive thoughts bring about positive response even to unpleasant actions. When you exhibit a strong positivity, you overpower the potential of any negative action around you.

HOW TO HANDLE CHALLENGE ELEGANTLY

Welcome it

Most of us don't experience the pleasure of solving problems because we are busy running away from them. Most challenges occur for a purpose, to build us, to test us, and to make us stronger. People that passed through the most challenges are the most experienced and tend to be unbent when it comes to social and emotional earthquakes. They are skilled in dealing with people and don't have to seek for shelter every time they feel someone is throwing a stone at them.

You don't have to be attached to a problem to solve it. The problem doesn't have to be a destructive problem before you take necessary action. You have to forget about your past failure and focus on today. Welcome the challenge and show it how good you can be. Once you start running, you will keep running all your life. Let stoutheartedness leads, and let your fears help you develop the right strategies to deal with problems.

It's okay to have negative people around you

Everyone has someone who is less-than-positive. You don't have to beat yourself up because you are facing a challenging situation with someone in the office. All that is needed from you is the courage to go through each day without breaking down. You don't even have to be a problem solver all the time. Focus your peace and let self-love lead the way. You learn more things from a low day than a good day.

Release the pressure

Seeking pleasure amidst a crisis is okay. Look for ways to deal with mental stress, comfortable to your state of mind. Avoid taking alcohol as much as possible. Opt-in for visualization, meditation, mindfulness, or any other relaxation technique that comes to mind. Sometimes taking a walk at the beach may provide the calmness needed. Taking a warm bath, or watching a good movie, alone, will provide the stillness needed for building strong positivity.

Let go of the pressure and do not allow work to affect your momentum when you set to relieve stress. Do this often, and you will never be frustrated about people or work.

Release the emotion

Feel what you are feeling and be honest about them. Suppressing your emotions are harmful to your mental wellbeing. Take the necessary steps to express your emotions, and do not hesitate to confront people when things are not going as they should be.

If you can't talk to anyone about your emotions at the time, punch something, shout, or take a walk. Release the tension in your muscles by running fast or having a vigorous exercise session. It is important to release every little tension to have a better judgment of things.

What are the sources of my problems?

People act for a reason. People are either acting or reacting to things around them.

Whenever you encounter a problem with someone, try and look for the source of the problem. Solving a problem at the surface will not lead to a permanent solution.

Who is the reason? What is the reason? What triggers such action or reaction?

Once you answer these questions, the source of the problem will be clear. So, you will worry less about what people are doing as a form of reaction, and focus on the solution, which will definitely impact their corresponding actions.

Most problems in the workplace sprout from long-term dissatisfaction. Look into that variable thoroughly, and you will have a good problem-solving perspective.

Take good care of yourself

You are your best tool. Take care of your emotional and physical health so you can deal with problems in the outside world. You must be nourished and physically capable of handling problems to avoid being crippled by challenges in your relationship or the workplace.

Cultivate good habits, exercise more, eat good food, and reduce or cut down on alcohol. Avoid unhealthy diet, avoid unhealthy people, and avoid unhealthy places. Never underestimate the power of exercising in keeping your body and mind fit. Exercise more and make good choices about what you put in your body, and you will be happy with yourself.

Know your surrounding

Your environment has big influences over your emotions and state of mind. The people you surround yourself with have an even bigger influence on your mindset. Your mood is influenced by how people approach you starting from your bed, the bus, office, and even playground.

Choose your environment carefully. You have more control over who to be with, than how they influence you. Constantly keeping negative people around you can only result in negativity. Surround yourself with people with whom you find relevance. They have to be interested in your progress and be fascinated by your charm. Do not surround yourself with people who don't appreciate you.

Do not confuse support with negative challenge. If they support you, they will challenge you to do better. If they don't support you, they will challenge you to bring you down. Choose wisely whom you choose to allow to influence your decisions when it comes to health, work, relationship, and emotions.

HOW TO PROTECT YOUR BOUNDARIES

Get Tough

A boundary violation is a common behavior of negative people. You don't have to let a violation slide. You don't have to fight them either. Make it clear to them that they have violated your personal space and that you don't expect them to repeat the same thing. Be stern and tough about it.

If you don't care much about yourself and your personal space, even the positive people will not give much thought about it. Do not assume that people will not violate your space just because it is the right thing to do. You have to define your space and explain exactly why you want them to be out of it.

Communicate your boundaries

Communicate your boundaries clearly. Sit people down and address them about what you want and what you dislike. Narrate clearly how you want things to be done, the limits and the consequences. Give them instructions on how they will respect you as a person. If you are not comfortable, tell them clearly. If you don't want to talk about something, be clear about the details. If you want to talk about something else, bring it to the table.

In all these, you don't have to give excuses and reasons to justify your need for boundaries. You don't need to answer questions if you don't want to.

Understand different boundaries and how they should be respected

Categorize your need for boundaries, so you don't confuse the violation for one with another. Develop a rule and principle considering how you want things to be done around you. Consider the following categories when making such rules:

Emotions: What someone else does should not affect your inner peace. Your actions are justified by your purpose, and you don't have to explain yourself to anyone.

Time: Your time is money, and no one should waste it. You have to learn to say NO sternly and never compromise your schedule just to please the next person. Take your time seriously, and people around you will respect it.

Space: How close does someone has to be to make you uncomfortable? There is no definite space for boundaries. Boundaries should be determined based on your level of comfort. Make a hint immediately you start getting uncomfortable with how close someone is getting.

Information: You have the right to have a private life. You are not obligated to share any information with people just for the sake of answering questions. Your medical or health details should only be shared with your doctor or loved ones. Your financial details could be shared with the ones that are concerned, in cases of usefulness. Information is a strong element that design your social outlook. Make sure you keep it safe and keep private what is private.

Possession: Your toothbrush is not the only personal item you shouldn't let others borrow. Keep track of the things you are not comfortable letting another person to use. To not hurt the feelings of the other person, look for a single reason you don't want to share, and no further explanation.

Also, some people have the habit of borrowing things and not returning them. In this case, know those people, and stop allowing them to borrow your stuff.

Money: This is a very important part of boundary creation. Know the amount of money you can lend to people, the amount you are willing to lose, and the amount you are willing to give out for free. Try as much as possible to reduce the rate at which you lend money to people.

Lending money often ruins relationships. If you can't dash it out, don't give it at all. Some may not have the means to repay, and some may take you for granted since you are friends. So, the best way to avoid complications and to keep the boundaries clear is to stop lending money.

Differentiate between genuine obligation and feeling obligated

Some people are good at making others feel obligated to do something. The best way to break out of the spell is to understand the difference between genuine and feeling obligation. Only do what needs to be done, without stressing yourself. Realize that what needs to be done is not always an obligation. Know your territory, your responsibilities, and try as much as possible to focus on your energy.

Be fast

Be fast in notifying the other person when they crossed your boundary. You don't have to be harsh. Just bring it to their attention how you want things to be done. Do not blame or complain, just state details of your preferred ways.

Sometimes people will cross your boundaries in the name of love. They might have good intentions, but always point out where you are not comfortable. Let the other person know your preference, and they will follow with love.

Set emotional boundaries

Do you notice that you do some things only when you are with this particular person? Do you notice that this person influences your unhealthy habits? Are you afraid that they will criticize you when you don't participate? Do they criticize you when you don't participate?

The first option is to cut this person off. The second option is to analyze the situation, to figure out the sources of your urge. Look into your fears and the need for approval. Make it clear to the person that you don't want to participate in such an act anymore. Also, stay away from anything that will trigger compulsive behavior.

What do you want?

Only do what you want, and what makes you feel comfortable. Meeting people's demands will cause stress and will eventually make you hate yourself and the people around you. Your sense of judgment will be impaired, and everything around you including people will look more negative than ever. So, whenever you are met with demand or commitment, ask yourself if you really want to do this thing. Know what you don't want to do, even when you are not busy.

Make a list

Make a list of people and relationships that bring about stress to your life. Include those relationships that you tend to be in a constant need to impress someone. There is no stress stronger than the feeling of inadequacy, and to constantly feel like you have to prove yourself before you will be considered or respected.

After making a list, analyze the relationship one by one according to the urges.

What are the sources of stress? Are you being pressurized? Do you just like working extra hard to feel better? Are you resenting this person? What is the exit strategy? Can you still make the relationship work without having to stress yourself?

Make a second list

The second list should contain activities and people that boost your energy. Look at the things that make your relationship pleasant, including the names of the people that make you happy. What is missing on the first list, that is very significant on the second list?

You will have a clear idea of using the second list as leverage for positivity and peace. Also, you can use the second list as a motivation to make the relationship of the first list work without inflicting stress to yourself.

The aim is to protect your energy; to increase your positive focus, and endeavor to create a safer environment for your emotional satisfaction.

IMPROVE YOUR SELF-ESTEEM

Your perceived self-esteem determines how much respect you will get from others. Negative or toxic people find it easier to oppress the weak ones. People with low self-esteem are weak and easy to exploit. There are several ways to boost your self-esteem and gain respect from others. You have to be honest with yourself, take the right action, and you will become the leader of your circle.

What makes you feel good?

Keep close what makes you feel good. Use visual or vocal reminders. You must own or accomplish these things, to have a true connection with them. Take pictures of yourself doing great things, collecting an award or just having fun with friends, and place them on your wall in the bedroom or office.

Put it up where you can see it and take pride in your accomplishments. Apart from boosting your self-esteem, you will develop ideas on what to do next. You will have a list of what you have not done yet, and pursue those things fearlessly.

Self-acceptance

Do not expect people to accept you for who you are if you don't accept yourself as you are. If you don't accept the person that is within you, and the person you can see in the physical, you will never have the confidence to express your feelings, thoughts, opinions or even to be among other people.

You should keep in mind that nobody is perfect and that you can improve with time. Even with your flaws, you are better than most people. So instead of overthinking about your weaknesses and imperfection, observe your environment and see how others are insecure and trying as much as possible to fit in.

Surround yourself with positive people

Low self-esteem is associated with long-term criticism from close friends and family.

If you don't surround yourself with people that appreciate you, you will always feel inadequate. Instead of pushing yourself to be at the 'cool-table,' stay around people who love and care about you.

Surround yourself with people who treat you like a king, and you will feel like a king everywhere you go. Keep your distance from people who don't see the good in you; who don't see how awesome you are as a person. You don't need many people in your life; you need just a few ones who appreciate you.

Do something new

Whenever you do something new, there is a boost in confidence and self-esteem. Knowing how to do one more thing means increasing your worth as a person. People who know how to do a lot of things have confidence because they know they always have something to offer.

Be too busy learning new things so that you will distract yourself from the thoughts and feelings of inadequacy. Learn web design, cooking, sewing, games, dance, art, music, etc. You will increase your value, even as you increase your income.

Change your perspective

Work on your perspectives when dealing with challenging situations. Instead of feeling responsible for things not going quite well, remove yourself from the picture. You will realize that even without you, things will still go bad. So, stop feeling sorry for yourself, and worry more about your wellbeing.

Be realistic about your expectations, and what people will actually believe or like. You are allowed to be creative and have big dreams, but always take each step with caution. The more positive thought you accumulate, the better you will carry out each given task, and you will achieve true satisfaction in the end.

Help someone

Generosity is one of the few secrets of boosting self-esteem often ignored by experts. Your level of self-worth is increased when you go out of your way to help someone, especially when you don't expect them to return the favor.

Being generous does not always mean giving out money. It could also mean giving someone your time, by listening to them or giving them good advice. When you become selfless, your confidence and self-esteem will improve. You will become bold in approaching others and dealing with problems.

Set real goals

People with goals don't even have time to drag their feet on the floor. Having goals means having a purpose. There is a reason you do what you do. You are not just wandering aimlessly, with no plans in mind. You have something in mind. You want to achieve something, and you are taking strategic steps to achieve those every day.

Make sure you are keeping track of your progress, and you are taking significant action every day to reach your goals. You will have a new challenge every day, and you will worry less about the challenge some irrelevant fellow will throw at you. You will focus only on good things, the good things you can do to yourself.

Take time off

Take time off to relax, away from all the hassles and demands of the common world. Creativity is very important in life. Without creativity, you will easily lose your balance; your purpose will begin to look blurry and uncertain.

Stress will make you feel sick, without knowing exactly what is wrong with you. When you feel sick, you won't have the energy to confront negative people, or even express your assertion clearly as a leader. Take a break, listen to music, play games, meditate, take a warm bath, etc., to put yourself to relaxation.

Take good care of yourself

Eat good food and exercise well. You don't have to work all day just because you need to prove yourself. Success is the best revenge, but health is the greatest wealth.

Do not betray your health just because you want to increase your social status. Wear good clothes and laugh with your loved ones. Don't be harsh on yourself, love yourself.

Take a long drive to feel the breeze. Do something crazy to cross over the hurdle of your insecurity. Dwell in the feeling of ecstasy, and make sure you enjoy it, because you deserve it.

Challenge negativity

Challenge any thought that will lead to depression or anxiety. Reward yourself on a little victory. Enjoy the benefit of delayed gratification, but always remember to reward yourself every day for sticking to the schedules, for overcoming a bad habit, and for thinking all day positively.

Keep the list of things you are grateful for in your pocket. Whenever you are feeling low, take the list out and read it aloud.

In boosting your self-esteem, you have to believe in your actions. You must believe that you can change and that you will gain respect when you take the necessary actions to build yourself. Never set the bar too low when it comes to how you want to be treated. The more trust you have in your abilities, the more trust people will have in you.

HOW TO EARN RESPECT

To completely get rid of negative people and attract positive people, who will eventually be the reason for your speedy elevation in life, you have to learn some respect strategies. You have to gain respect in such a way you will become scary to negative people and mediocrity.

It is time to upgrade your standards and social circle.

It is time to start attracting better things, and better people.

It is time to inspire yourself to grow and allow only positive people who will further encourage you to be the best you can be.

Control your emotions

To earn respect, you have to be in control of your reaction when you are upset and when you are happy. Do not make decisions when you are excited or angry. Keep your emotions in check and only express them with class. Be enthusiastic as much as possible, but instead of reacting, respond.

Work on your empathic skills

Develop a high level of empathy. Develop good listening skills and find a way to show others that you understand them. People respect and depend on people whom they think understand them. You will begin to look reliable and strong. Always be there for others when they need you the most. If you can't be there, delegate, and use all the control you have to make them feel valued.

Talk less

If you can bring to mind one prominent and respected person you know, you will realize that this person doesn't talk much. They only speak when necessary and often prove themselves by taking actions.

Instead of talking, actively listen to the next person. Be a good listener, and people will label you as a good conversationalist. Only speak when you have something sensible or valuable.

Voice out your opinion

Let your opinion be clear. If you have an idea about something, let it out. People respect you when you have an undeterred opinion about something. It keeps them wondering about the source of your wisdom. If you have an idea about the better ways of handling things, let the world know. You have to be strong like a leader to be perceived as one.

Be dependable

Be the person someone else can rely on for protection or support. Learn to stand for people who can't stand for themselves. You know when you are strong, and when you can handle a problem. It doesn't have to be something big, just focus on being a good person.

Guide your territory

Be clear about boundaries and confront anyone who crosses yours. Do not be passive about negative people. Whenever you feel taken advantage of, speak up and let them know their wrongs. Even though you may need to be diplomatic, always let them know that you cannot be a doormat, not even for a second.

Trust your plans

People don't get respected because they have self-doubt. You have ideas, and you should believe in them. All the strategies or patterns people are following today is another person's ideas. If you think you have something better, don't be afraid to implement them. Don't be afraid to tell people to try them. Creative people gain respect because they always have amazing ideas and they are bold to share.

Don't criticize

You are free to criticize others but stop criticizing yourself. Negative self-talk is one of the strongest killers of self-confidence. No one will respect you if you lack self-confidence. You may have some doubts, it's okay, but never underestimate your abilities to do exploits. You may fail, but learn the lessons and take the next step.

Inspire others

Be a motivation in your little ways. Be confident of your success and take each step with grace. Be passionate about your goals and dreams. Take amazing steps and never stop seeking for betterment. Encourage others to do the same. Show them that you believe in them and that they could do better.

Bring something to the table

Respect is all about the amount of value you bring to the table or at least, the amount of perceived value. Value doesn't have to be materialistic or monetary. You can add motivational value, work value or insightful value. On the other hand, helping others to finish their work, getting things done when the person responsible is incapable, are other ways to add value.

CONCLUSION

Keep working on yourself to become a stronger and better version of you. Let your experience become a lesson, and let the knowledge obtained become a tool for social excellence.

Learn to become effective in every aspect of life. Develop self-love and people will love and respect you. Your life will repel negativity, and you will begin to attract people of the same mindset. In social circles, likes attract likes. So, be open-minded and have a defined moral code.

Be humble but not too nice. Be elegant and sophisticated in your moves. Never think less of yourself, no matter the situation. Be bold enough to show yourself as the person that you are.

Stay away from gossip and spend your time cultivating better habits. Do not allow unserious people to waste your time. Stop apologizing and be relentlessly proactive.

Other Books by The Same Author

Change Your Life: How to Overcome Anxiety, Depression and Negative Thinking

Anxiety and Phobia Workbook: How to Overcome Anxiety and Panic Attacks

How to Deal with Difficult People: Control the Situation! Overcome Your Annoying and Frustrating Coworkers, Friends, Parents, or Classmates

How to Overcome Shyness and Social Anxiety: Deal with Stage Fright, Fear of Public Speaking, Social Phobia, And Ultimately Gain New Confidence

How to Deal with Rejection: Powerful Ways to Restore Social Confidence, Attract Better Opportunities, And Take Charge of Your Environment

How to Deal with A Narcissist: Best Ways to Respond to A Narcissist,

Confront Self-Important People, And Thrive Efficiently

Anger Management Techniques: How to Control Outbursts, Frustration, & Depression Using Emotional Intelligence

www.ingramcontent.com/pod-product-compliance
Lightning Source LLC
Chambersburg PA
CBHW020618220526
45463CB00006B/2615